CHIC
SIMPLE ®
Components

"The palest ink is better than the best memory."

CHINESE PROVERB

CHIC
SIMPLE ®
Components

D E S K

ALFRED A. KNOPF NEW YORK 1994

THIS IS A BORZOI BOOK
PUBLISHED BY ALFRED A. KNOPF, INC.

KIM JOHNSON GROSS   JEFF STONE

WRITTEN BY TODD LYON
PHOTOGRAPHS BY DANA GALLAGHER
ILLUSTRATIONS BY GREGORY NEMEC
STYLED BY SUSAN CLAIRE MALONEY

ART DIRECTION BY WAYNE WOLF
ICON ILLUSTRATION BY ERIC HANSON

Library of Congress Cataloging-in-Publication Data
Gross, Kim Johnson.
Chic simple desk /[Kim Johnson Gross, Jeff Stone;
written by Todd Lyon].
p. cm. — (Chic simple components)
ISBN 0-679-43220-5
1. Office equipment and supplies. 2. Desks. 3. Office decoration.
I. Stone, Jeff, [date]. II. Lyon, Todd. III. Title. IV. Series.
HF5547.G795 1994
651'.2—dc20
94-28900
CIP

Manufactured in the United States of America
First Edition

CONTENTS

THE DESK

A brief history of work surfaces; the desk as helpmate, playmate, and kitchen table; the disappearing desk, the simple desk

11

WORK SPACE

Optional environments: ergonomics, electronics, desks that stay and desks that don't, places to sit, read, file, and fret

37

EQUIPMENT

Desktop dramatics; movable type; small pleasures

63

FIRST AID

Need some help in the office? How about software and hard facts?

86

WHERE

Worldwide destinations for the desktop shopper

91

"The more you know, the less you need."

AUSTRALIAN ABORIGINAL SAYING

CHIC
SIMPLE ®

Chic Simple is a primer for living well but sensibly. It's for those who believe that quality of life does not come in accumulating things, but in paring down to the essentials. Chic Simple enables readers to bring value and style into their lives with economy and simplicity.

D E S K

The desk picks up where our bodies leave off. Like a vanity, it lets us see ourselves; like a partner, we bounce ideas off it; like a bed, we hunker down in it and get lost. It is no more just an object with four legs and six drawers than offices are just places where work gets done. Our true desk may be a mixing-board in a recording studio, a sketchpad in a field, a light-box in an x-ray room. The word itself is a kind of shorthand for that quiet place where we may concentrate, where we may store ideas like energy.

"Be regular and orderly in your life like
a bourgeois, so that you may be violent and
original in your work."

FLAUBERT

THE HISTORY OF THE DESK
HAS MADE A CIRCLE AND HAS COME

AROUND TO GREET ITSELF AGAIN. THE FIRST DESKS, after all, were slabs of stone and clay on which pictographs were carved; they were both desk and tablet, a place to write and a permanent record. In basic form and function, those slabs are an awful lot like laptop computers. But it's been a long journey. Parchment and papyrus were carried in portable writing-boxes; paper, invented in China, stayed close to the floor until it came West, where chair-sitters needed elevated surfaces to accommodate scrolls and balance bottles of ink. Today, the European influence shows itself in weighty, many-drawered desks, and delicate writing tables. But the microchip has rapidly removed the need for right-angled surfaces, and the desk is again a portable slab on which modern hieroglyphs may be entered and stored.

"He and I had an office so tiny that an inch smaller and it would have been adultery."

DOROTHY PARKER

FUNDAMENTAL EQUIPMENT

American settlers used wooden boxes with slanted tops as desks. They were called "Bible boxes" because they often held the family's one and only book.

FRACTURED FRANGLAIS

*The French had a practice of covering desk boxes with wool (*bure*); thus, the word "bureau" came to signify any desk compartment. It was later corrupted in America to mean "chest of drawers."*

BILLETS-DOUX

During Louis XV's reign, a rage for letter- and memoir-writing prompted the popularity of the small "lady's desk," a fussy writing table that became a standard feature in better French homes.

> "There is a widespread feeling
> that just because a man has a large
> office, he must be an idiot."

MR. NORTON, *Double Indemnity, 1944*

Functional Desk. Question: What has four legs, one surface, and functions as a communications center, a filing system, an art studio, a clerical workstation, a changing table, and a place to play cards on Wednesday nights? Answer: The average desk. Some desks, of course, have more specific functions. A CEO may lean back in a leather chair, behind a small empire of gleaming mahogany. But a one-piece school desk, battered and scuffed and stuck with gum, serves an equally important function. The painter's easel is a desk of sorts; and who can say that a wall, strewn with papers and thumbtacks, is any less than a vertical desk?

14

Personality. The best offices are mental playgrounds, but some offices are not offices at all. Marcel Proust's bed became his office, with a "desk" of three nightstands stocked with books, pens, hot-water bottles, and handkerchiefs. When Diana Vreeland inherited Condé Nast's gigantic office at *Vogue*, she promptly installed a partition because she couldn't "sit at a desk and watch someone walk for that length of time into a room." The moral: Ask not if your office works; ask how well your office makes *you* work.

WHO ARE YOU? *Cecil Williams and associates of Herman Miller, Inc., developed a system, using the Myers-Briggs Type Indicator, to identify and accommodate personal working styles.* **VISIONARIES** *are achievers who focus on the future while subordinating human elements. They need storage for reference materials, lots of privacy, and space.* **CATALYSTS** *are serious about information but try to make everyone happy. Their ideal work environments have bulletin boards, areas to receive visitors, and plenty of desk space for "filing."* **STABILIZERS** *want logical rules so that a business can essentially run itself. They should have easy access to information, and electronic equipment for storing data.* **COOPERATORS** *are practical and work with enthusiasm once they understand what is expected of them.*

Personal Desk. There are two kinds of working. The first is the kind that talks on the telephone. It involves marketing ideas, making a living. The second kind of working has no clock. Krishnamurti writes of its interflow, when "the division between the outer and the inner comes to an end." Those who write letters and books, those who invent and visualize, wish for the second kind of work. It can't be counted on but must be planned for nonetheless. Equip yourself so you can work until dawn and beyond.

THE SECRETARY *In Victorian times, covering up was so important that letters, papers, bills—the messy underthings of household business—were locked away in a secret desk, a.k.a. secretary. Disguised as a piece of furniture, the flat front opened (with a key) while the board itself became a writing surface. Future variations included the rolltop—once known as the "curtain-top"—and the fall front.*

WHERE THEY WORKED *Thomas Wolfe wrote on top of an icebox. Thomas Jefferson, Winston Churchill, and Ernest Hemingway all worked standing up. The Duke of Windsor's "desk" was a wooden board placed over the tub in his bathroom. Samuel Clemens's library, built to his exact specifications, had such a nice view that he had to move to a plainer room, where he worked facing the wall.*

The Pencil. Thank Henry David Thoreau for putting the American pencil on the map. From the 1600s on, domestic pencils were "greasy, gritty, brittle, inefficient" instruments that didn't compare to the fine pencils made in Germany and France. Then, in the mid-1800s, Thoreau quit his Massachusetts teaching job, went to

work for his pencil-making dad, and invented a clay and graphite mix that, by 1847, made Thoreau & Co. pencils among the best in the world. When Henry D. quit the business and escaped to Walden Pond, Ralph Waldo Emerson was outraged: "Instead of engineering for all America," wrote Emerson, "he was the captain of a huckleberry-party."

ONE PERSON'S FAVORITE

*According to connoisseur Henry Petroski, pencil pundits favor the
FaberCastell Velvet, the Berol Mirado No. 2, and the Faber Blackwing ("half the
pressure, twice the speed").*

ANOTHER'S FAVORITE

*Introduced in 1849, the Eberhard Faber Mongol was the first pencil
to be painted yellow; it features 13 coats of paint and claims a potential output
of 45,000 words per pencil. The authors of* Quintessence *call it
"the very best pencil there is."*

"You're as sensual as a pencil."

FRANK N. FURTER,

The Rocky Horror Picture Show, 1975

Computer Desk. Bauhaus via Kmart has loosened its ugly grip on computer tables. Components that were once stacked in military formations have scattered: The printer's in the closet and the hard drive is on the floor, slim as a greyhound and twice as loyal. For what's left, designers have built sexy new homes. Some are butlers that quietly retreat into the background of your eclectic office. Others straddle you like a lover who only wishes to serve. The new computer furniture is whimsical, curvaceous, and built to accommodate the practical and aesthetic needs of hardworking homebodies.

> "Something in me believes that my typewriter has a soul similar to Dorothy Parker's, and that it's proud of me every time I type something clever."
>
> CYNTHIA HEIMEL

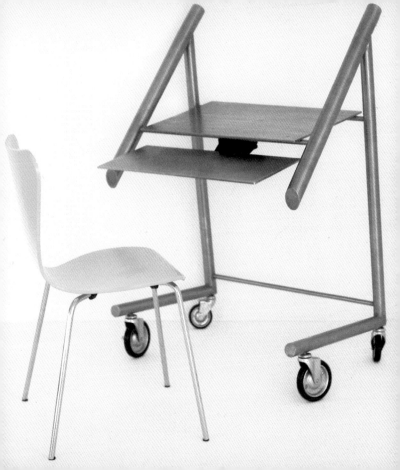

VERSATILITY   *To eat surrounded by books, to work with flatware and place mats within reach, is an arrangement that suits the modern condition. With files on casters we could roll our tasks from room to room; or we could flip our Murphy desk into the wall when company comes; or we could set up a folding card table in the backyard. But it's still the kitchen table we are drawn to—to stand around at parties, to do our taxes, write our letters, dream our dreams on paper.*

"All I needed was a steady table and a typewriter...
a marble-topped bedroom washstand table made a good
place; the dining-room table between meals
was also suitable."

AGATHA CHRISTIE

Portable Desk. Neatness-nut Jeffrey Mayer advises, "If you would really like to improve your daily productivity and take control of your telephone calls, to-do's, meetings and appointments…put your personal organizer inside your computer." He's referring, of course, to personal information managers (PIMs), the programs that convert date books, addresses, and scribbled reminders into sleek, paper-free data. Now the PIM has gone beyond basics and evolved into the Personal Digital Assistant, a small wonder that can manage your calendar, make lists, create reminders. More than a portable desk, it's a portable office, without the coffee.

SIGNATURE SERIES

For years, people (like your dad) who never learned to type have been hunting and pecking with two fingers. Look out: Here come pen computers, those palmtop pals equipped with handwriting-recognition software. The best known are the Apple Newton and the Sharp Wizard. On them one can take notes or write letters with a penlike instrument, then file or fax them away.

Now people (like your dad) with illegible handwriting will have to work on their penmanship.

Eraser. "I NEVER MAKE MISTEAKS." It was a phrase emblazoned on joke erasers. It made the rounds in elementary school, during the same era when older teachers referred to erasers as "gums." A "misteak," we were sure, but no: The teachers were just remembering a time when erasers were made from gum elastic or "India rubber," a tree resin. With New Math came un-gumlike erasers, designed to suit specific instruments and applications. Soft vinyl erasers are made for soft-lead pencils used on paper and film; certain plastic models are made for erasing ink. But the pink erasers that top writing pencils have a secret life: They're also great as earring backs.

Virtual Desk. Ever since computers began to shrink the world, the desk-as-metaphor has been central to software programming. There is the macro view: Tasks that once required dozens of employees and a fleet of offices can now be carried out on a single computer. So a desk is not a desk but the symbol of an intimate, one-on-one relationship in a small space. But for software writers there is a second meaning. A desktop is also the live area on a computer monitor. Within that miniature theatre one can edit, file, do research, write books, create graphics, get organized. It is a virtual office, and in spite of the fact that its physical measurements may be slight, it is vastly larger than the literal desktop it occupies.

"Computers are useless. They can only give you answers."

PABLO PICASSO

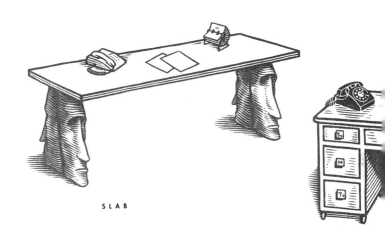

SLAB

Desk Types. The PEDESTAL desk was inspired by the 18th-century library table; it's the traditional, symmetrical desk with front-facing drawers along each side. As if a place to put one's legs were a startling innovation, pedestals are sometimes called KNEEHOLE desks. The PARTNERS desk is good for people who either really like each other or

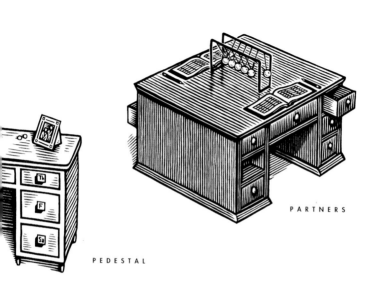

PARTNERS

PEDESTAL

don't trust each other at all. It allows for the love/hate-birds to sit face to face and access drawers that open on either side. The SLAB desk evolved from the pedestal, but you'd never know it; today, it is any modular unit featuring a work surface (Formica, glass, plywood) stabilized on a pair of bases (filing cabinets, glass bricks, sawhorses, canned goods).

Simple Desk. The wicked Viscount in *Les Liaisons Dangereuses* was forever taking up his quill pen to write love letters in bed. For a desk he used the naked back of his latest conquest. Although an interesting solution, backs do have their bumps; a flatter alternative is the inanimate lap desk. There are official lap desks with smooth tops and beanbag bottoms, but any old board will do. A large book can be a lap desk; so can a briefcase on a train, a clipboard, or a reporter's notebook on the run. A laptop computer is a window to a world of information but in essence it's still a lap desk, the passive guest at a party for two.

YOUR FIRST DESK
Bright plastic desk with hinged top for hours of opening-and-slamming-shut fun

YOUR SECOND THROUGH TWELFTH DESK
One-piece molded number with chrome tubing, chair attached (preferably beige)

YOUR COMING-OF-AGE DESK
Hollow-core door laid across plastic milk crates pilfered from the supermarket

YOUR FUTURE DESK
Channel 421 on your television

W O R K   S P A C E

A place to sit and think, a surface on which to make nota-
tions, keep records, maintain momentum: This is all we
need to do our work. It doesn't have to be pretty, nor does
it have to match. Architects and interior designers have
many stories about the client for whom they created a
magnificent office, impeccably outfitted with built-in everything, which was soon abandoned because the client
preferred to scribble at a coffee table in front of the TV.

"The tools I need for my work are paper,
tobacco, food and a little whiskey."

WILLIAM FAULKNER

Ergonomics. Although introduced as early as 1925, the study of the relationship between humans and machines only became vital when widespread computer use spawned an epidemic of CTDs, or cumulative trauma disorders. Carpal tunnel syndrome, eyestrain, back pain, and tendonitis—the best-known CTDs—now account for 50 percent of all illnesses in the workplace. The situation is severe enough that, as early as 1990, the city of San Francisco passed a law requiring employers to provide computer operators with non-glare task lighting, detachable computer keyboards, and monitors that are height and angle adjustable.

1. Keyboard wrist rest
2. Mouse wrist pad

SURF'S UP
Stephen Peart has designed everything from wet suits to Apple's Adjustable Keyboard. Now his passion is ergonomic accessories— wrist rests, mouse pads, foot- and backrests—in "functional biomorphic shapes." The series of puddle-shaped objects is named "Surf" and is designed to ease the rigid geometry of computer use.

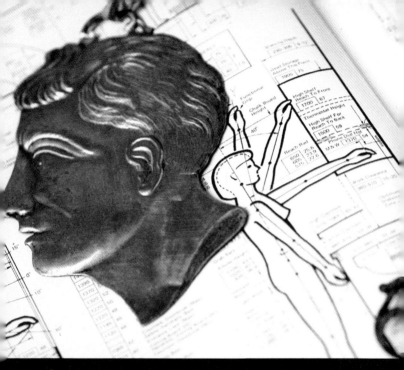

THE ERGONOMIC OFFICE

1. To decrease neck pain and eyestrain, position your computer monitor so that the top of the screen is level with your forehead, 18 to 20 inches from your face. 2. Position your forearms at 90-degree angles to your elbows and keep your wrist angle below 10 degrees. This position has been shown to reduce incidences of carpal tunnel syndrome. 3. Use a padded wrist rest. 4. Perform stretching and breathing exercises as often as ● 15 minutes.

POISON TABLE

The word "credenza" comes from the Latin credere, to trust. In ancient times, a credenza was a table where food was placed to be tasted for poison before it was served. Today it simply holds all those things your desk can't, including the occasional poisonous memo.

Environment. "If you're going to withdraw into yourself," wrote Montaigne in the 16th century, "first prepare yourself a welcome." For writing letters and paying bills, a sun-flooded corner with a comfortable chair may be welcome enough;

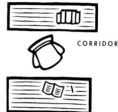

CORRIDOR

for more complicated tasks, consider a traditional office setup. The

STRAIGHT-LINE style is one in which desk and equipment is set up in a single row against a long wall. The

ELL features a task table set at right angles to a desk,

STRAIGHT LINE

while the CORRIDOR style has a long table or credenza placed parallel to a desk so that a swivel chair may move along the "corridor" in between. Don't be afraid to mix it up.

ELL

Electronics. The microchip is almost 40 years old; the personal computer is nearly 20. The two have spawned electronic conveniences beyond the wildest imaginations of '50s futurists, which may explain why many of our homes have electrical systems appropriate for '50s technology. When planning your office space, get basic: Count your outlets first. Before installing the computer, the fax, the modem, the printer, the scanner, the answering machine, the battery charger for the cordless telephone, the lamps, and the clock, you may want to contact your friendly neighborhood electrician or power station.

YOUR PLACE OUT OF THE SUN *Computer terminals should be kept out of direct sunlight and positioned so that the system's cooling fans—located on three sides—are completely unobstructed. Likewise, keep it away from devices that create strong magnetic fields, like transformers, electric motors, speakers, or fans.*

TOWER OF POWER *Computers, fax machines, printers, and modems all require surge-protected electrical outlets. Modems are especially vulnerable to high-voltage damage, but even the best surge protector can't prevent damage from an electrical storm. All electronic equipment should be unplugged when lightning seems likely.*

THE SOUL OF AN OLD MACHINE *"Vintage" computers—that is, models from the '70s—are being rescued from scrap metal piles and purchased by collectors. The Apple I, which was introduced in 1976 and sold for $666.66, can now fetch as much as $12,000. Who would of have thought it?*

Chair. In *Made in the U.S.A.*, Phil Patton wrote, "The quintessential American chair is, of course, the rocker. Like chewing gum or whittling, the rocking chair sums up our national restlessness." But if restlessness were the standard, it could be better argued that office chairs are Most American. They move back and forth, spin around, zoom on casters, and get taller or shorter with the push of a little lever. Office rock 'n' roll.

CHOOSING AN ERGONOMIC OFFICE CHAIR

Look for: 1. *Adjustable height* 2. *Lumbar support in the form of a curve built into the lower part of the backrest* 3. *A tilt feature that allows you to lean forward and backward while keeping your feet on the floor* 4. *Adjustable armrests to take weight off your neck and shoulders* 5. *Width and height to support your shoulders and head.*

Uni-ball.

Sleek as a Stealth bomber
and functional as a clothespin, the Uni-
ball®—generically called a roller ball—takes the
Industrial Age's promise of affordability, dependability, and ele-
gance, and signs it in ink. Once upon a time, roller ball pens had water-
based ink and ballpoint pens had oil-based ink. It was the only differ-
ence between the two, as they had the same ball-in-socket design. Now
the Eberhard Faber Uni-ball XL features archival-quality waterproof
ink, perfect for signing checks and writing addresses in the rain. Its metal
point and fine to microfine stroke puts the Uni-ball somewhere between
the high-maintenance fountain pen and the giveaway ballpoint, while
its flat black casing makes it a classic addition to any pen wardrobe.

600,000 TO 3000 B.C.: *Pointy rocks, bones, flints.*

5000 TO 2500 B.C.: *Needles of bone or metal (the stylus); iron chisels (for carving pictographs).*

2500 B.C. TO A.D. 300: *Reed pens, bamboo pens, brushes dipped in a carbon/gum solution.*

A.D. 300 TO 1806: *Goose feather quills, dipped in ink.*

1806: *Pen holders fitted with metal nibs.*

1850: *Fountain pens, lever on side.*

1949: *Ballpoint pens.*

1972: *Ballpoint pens, unthreatened by felt tip pens.*

1994: *Ballpoint pens, unthreatened by roller ball pens.*

Let There Be Lighting. Walls don't have to define a work area. A desk, a chair, and a pool of light can become an office in wide-open spaces. Two kinds of lighting are essential: GENERAL, or ambient, lighting provides overall visibility; TASK lighting provides direct illumination of the job at hand. For general lighting, commercial offices use fluorescent bulbs because they give more bang, wattage-wise, for the buck. But fluorescents are cold, cruel to the complexion, and too bright. Concentration is best when general lighting is dimmer than task lighting; try floor lamps with incandescent bulbs turned heavenward. Task lighting is divided into two types: SYMMETRICAL, which distributes light evenly in all directions, and ASYMMETRICAL, which concentrates light in a single direction. When using a computer, asymmetrical lights are preferred, because they can point light away from the glowing monitor and illuminate only the work area instead.

Luxo Stuff. In the late 1920s an English manufacturer invented an adjustable lamp that he called the Anglepoise. Its stripped, skeletal design drew the attention of Norwegian industrialist Jac Jacobsen; he bought the patent, made some adjustments, and the Luxo, so named for the luxury of its fully directional light, was born. Immediately adopted by designers everywhere, the Luxo reached icon status when it became the subject of an award-winning computer-animated film, *Luxo, Jr.* Lately, ergonomic concerns have spawned a new breed of Luxos including Halogen Task Lighting Systems 1 and 2 and the Jac, an asymmetric task lamp.

LAMP LORE

1. *Flex-arm lamps should be placed at a far corner of your desk so that light shines diagonally but the bare bulb is shaded.* 2. *Task lamps with both incandescent and fluorescent bulbs give the truest color reading.* 3. *To cut down on eyestrain when working with a monitor, keep soft background lights illuminated at all times.* 4. *To see clearly in a working situation, a 40-year-old requires twice as much light as a 20-year-old; a 60-year-old requires four to five times what a 20 year-old needs.*

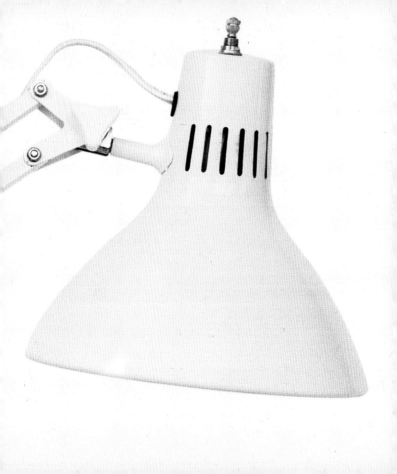

Organization. January 10 is national "Clean Off Your Desk Day." Some people don't need it. Mother Teresa, for instance, has a desk in her Calcutta office that has nothing on it but a telephone. Albert Einstein, on the other hand, was so disorganized he became famous for losing paychecks—they'd turn up years later between the pages of books, where he'd used them to mark his place. To the Einstein-inclined, loose memos and piles of unfinished work are like a horizontal bulletin board and serve as visual reminders of tasks ahead. But the Mother Teresas of the world are driven mad by clutter. They require serenity and closure at the end of the day, i.e., polished and paper-free work environments. Which is where organizational equipment comes in handy.

"I must create a system, or be enslaved by another man's."

WILLIAM BLAKE

CLUTTER QUOTA

The average office worker generates 45 sheets of paper a day, spends 3 hours a week looking for things, and will allow 36 hours of work to pile up on his or her desk.

ORGANIZED CLUTTER

Expanding accordion files, pasteboard portfolios tied with ribbon, manila folders, clasp envelopes, three-ring binders... boxes that remember pumps, or Whitman's long-ago "Sampler"s... chemical-free beakers, terra-cotta pots in which no flowers grow....

PASS THE CLUTTER

In the mid 1920s Emile-Jacques Ruhlmann designed a desk for the Maharaja of Indore. The ebony, fan-shaped desk featured five "out" baskets under the desk's surface, each partly covered with a piece of heavy glass, so that papers could be routed to the Maharaja's five principalities.

HISTORICAL CLUTTER

Thomas Jefferson had an octagonal filing table at Monticello; each of its eight drawers were labeled with three consecutive letters of the alphabet.

GO FIGURE

When setting up office in China, remember that the Chinese language has no alphabet and therefore no logical system for organizing filing systems—or dictionaries and encyclopedias, for that matter.

*The Gem paper clip had its
beginnings about 1900; its
bent-wire design is still the
paper-clip standard.*

The Paper Clip. There

are plenty of stories as to how the paper

clip came to be. The prettiest one is this: In 1899

a Norwegian named Johan Vaaler invented a single-wire

device that could clip papers together, a revolutionary idea, since

until then straight pins had done the task. With no patent laws in

Norway, Vaaler sought a patent in Germany. But the Norwegians remem-

bered the origin of the clip and, under occupation during World War II,

wore them on their lapels in a show of patriotism. This so irritated the

Germans that the wearing of paper clips became punishable by arrest.

CLIP NOTES

Plastic-coated clips are good for computer users as they block magnetic fields.

Ridged clips have increased holding power and are especially useful on slippery fax paper.

The Owl clip has double loops and, with a stretch of the imagination, looks vaguely like the animal for which it is named.

The Ideal clip looks like origami; its wide gripping area is designed to hold large numbers of sheets.

The flat-mouth clamp that can turn any piece of cardboard into a clipboard is known as the Bulldog.

Binder clips come in dozens of sizes; they're the black spring steel clamps with the folding wire wings.

Files. Electronic helpers may lighten its load, but as long as bills are sent through the mail, notes are scribbled on pads, and hard copy makes the rounds, the filing cabinet will not budge from its prominent place on the office floor. We can squirrel our papers away in a VERTICAL file, which is the quintessential front-to-back-in-a-drawer option; a HANGING file, in which folders may be grouped within larger dividers that hang suspended from tracks; a LATERAL system, which stores files side by side for better visual access (and an increase in active floor space); or we can BIND our files and shelve them like books, in the European tradition.

I BEG YOU TO BURN

Cardboard files are convenient and portable, oak filing cabinets are lovely, but neither are fireproof—unless they're metal-lined. Metal cabinets are essential for flammable materials such as rubber cement, thinners, oil-based paints, and bourbon. Certain wily writers, fearing for the safety of original manuscripts, store important papers in the refrigerator.

FILE STYLE

The metal flat file is excellent for storing large documents, like architectural drawings, and can double as a coffee table—just add a slab of glass.

Bigger Than a Breadbox. Information is always being compressed into smaller and smaller spaces. This frees up a lot of room for houseplants and knickknacks, but can be confusing to already bewildered consumers—we who are still baffled by The Clapper. Once the facts are grasped, however, it's liberating to know that, should we ever need to store 523 filing cabinets' worth of information, we don't have to rent a warehouse. We can, instead, slip a little DAT tape, smaller than an audio cassette tape, into a trench-coat pocket. Unfortunately, it also means we can now easily misplace 523 filing cabinets.

ROMANCING THE ROM

When attempting to visualize the CD-ROM storage capacity, picture this: One program called "Redshift" allows you to hang suspended 10,000 miles above Earth, travel under Saturn's rings, visit Halley's Comet, access the Penguin Dictionary of Astronomy, *and read on-screen panels of astronomical data. Storage-wise, that's a lot of shoe boxes.*

1	14.7	523	523
DAT (Digital Audio Tape)	**CD-ROM** (Read-Only Memory)	3.5-inch disk	Two-drawer filing cabinet

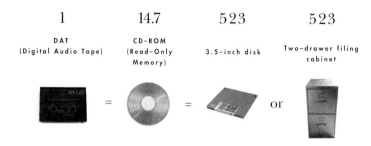

SIZE MATTERS

DAT (DIGITAL AUDIO TAPE) Can store up to 10 gigabytes (1,000 megabytes = one gigabyte). DAT tapes are used as back-up storage because information can only be stored or retrieved from them. Data has to be brought into a computer's hard drive in order to be read. **CD-ROM (READ-ONLY MEMORY)** Can store 680 megabytes. Like DAT tape, CD-ROMs are for information storage and retrieval. **3.5-INCH DISK** Average capacity is 1.3 megabytes. Though often referred to as a "floppy disk," 3.5-inch disks are in fact hard-shelled. Data can be created, edited, and deleted on the disk itself. **TWO-DRAWER FILING CABINET** Entire contents may be stored on a single 3.5-inch disk. It's true that a floppy disk and a filing cabinet are equal in storage but a door thrown over the top of two floppies makes a lousy desk.

E Q U I P M E N T

Every generation has its desk accessories. Some are dictated by technology and become defunct within a decade (remember the eraser-on-a-wheel with attached brush?). But others—those that combine beauty, function, and exquisite engineering—will never be abandoned on the side of the Information Highway.

"If all that survives of our fatally flawed civilization is the humble paper clip, archaeologists from some galaxy far, far away may give us more credit than we deserve."

OWEN EDWARDS

MAGIC RUB®
MEIF Eberhard Faber· 1954

Federnschachtel
beinhaltet 12 Stück, allerbeste
Schreibfedern verschiebener Herkunft.
ABRASAN·BASEL/SCHWEIZ

THE BIRTH OF THE POST-IT

When Post-it note pads hit the market in the mid 1980s, everyone from students to secretaries developed amnesia—no one could remember how we possibly managed without them. Except for Art Fry, a 3M engineer. He was singing in his church choir in 1974 when the scraps of paper he used as bookmarks fell to the floor. Divinely inspired, Fry experimented with an "unglue" that a colleague had developed at 3M and found a formula that temporarily stuck but didn't harm the pages of his hymnal. It took 10 years to convince 3M that the product was worthy of marketing; now Post-its are so universal that they're even made in long strips to accommodate Japanese writing.

Fetishes. One of the pleasures of having your very own desk is that you can heap it with miniature playmates. DESK SETS are those units, antique or highly modern, that feature a pen, an inkwell, and a small box in which to stash nibs and stamps. LETTER OPENERS are another discreet indulgence; once you're in the habit of using one, your digits seem hopelessly clumsy. Anything can become a PENCIL CUP; an empty can of Popeye's spinach or a simple clay pot will do. PAPERWEIGHTS, being virtually useless, are the most fun of all. How about a snow shaker, a meteorite, a Mystic 8-Ball? (Yes. No. Try again later.)

THE PAPER TRAIL

BEFORE A.D. 105: *Paper is invented in China, and travels to Samarkand; Arabs bring it to North Africa and Moors carry it on their conquests.* **A.D. 110:** *The first European paper mill is established in Xativa, Spain.* **1348:** *Mills appear in France.* **1300s:** *Watermarks are used to identify papermakers and/or to signify religious affiliation.* **1690:** *The first American paper mill opens in Germantown, Pa.* **1720:** *A French naturalist observes that wasps' nests are made from a paperlike substance. His studies lead to experimental papers made from pine cones, grass, and, finally, trees.* **1801:** *While trying to meet a market demand for wallpaper, Frenchman Nicholas-Louis Robert invents a papermaking machine. It revolutionizes the paper industry, which had been producing sheets of paper by hand.*

Paper. The paperless office was a dream of mid-century futurists, who envisioned an environment of sleek machines and no waste. But the cool digital world, rather than threatening paper with extinction, has made it seem ever richer by comparison. At Tiffany & Co., Cartier, and other arbiters of taste, sales of writing paper have increased while standards of quality have remained princely. Tiffany's watermarked papers still come in ecru, white, gray, or blue only; at Cartier's, the most correct stationery set will always be white rag paper with hand-painted gray borders and fully lined, bordered envelopes.

Pen. Throughout history the process of inking was so tedious that pens, penknives, ink, and drying powders were reserved for only the most final of documents. The earliest first drafts were etched on animal skins, then traced over with reed pens. Wax-covered wooden tablets, popular as early as 3000 B.C., reappeared in the Middle Ages; it's believed that Chaucer composed *The Canterbury Tales* on these, carving words out of the wax with the sharp end of a metal stylus and smoothing out errors with the blunt end. (The stylus was a mean weapon, too: In a heated senate debate, Caesar used his to stab Cassius in the arm.) Leonardo da Vinci drew in silverpoint on pumice-coated paper, then inked his drawings with a quill pen. Eventually, goose quills and metal nibs were placed in penholders, but it wasn't until the 1850s, when the fountain pen was invented, that nib, casing, ink, and ink supply were merged into a single unit. Oh pen, if thou art handy and portable, can ballpoints be far behind?

"The pen of my dream is a golden pen; it g
parchment; it is dipped into a crystal well of ink bla
fine as those which Indian art

JOHN MIDDLETON M

over a great sheet of white paper like crisp
than a raven's breast; and the lines it traces are as
draw with an elephant's hair."

"The Golden Pen"

Ink. It has been with us since 2500 B.C. or so, when it was simultaneously invented in China and Egypt. It's barely changed a drop since. Though we now have clog-free inks that flow freely through modern pens, India ink—the dense black fluid preferred by artists and calligraphers—is virtually the same stuff that was used in the second century. In China and Japan ink is still sold in solid blocks, and traditionalists still practice the ancient ritual of rubbing the block with water until the solid ink dissolves into a puddle of pure blackness. Like paint, ink is either water-based or oil-based. Ballpoint pens, permanent markers, and technical pens generally hold oil-based ink, while fountain pens, felt tip pens, and roller balls are usually loaded with water-based ink.

> "Ink is the cosmetic that ideas will wear when they go out in public. Graphite is their dirty truth."
>
> HENRY PETROSKI

Movable Type. There is nothing mysterious about the origins of movable type: It was invented by Bi Sheng, in China, in 1045, and involved characters made from clay. So much for Johann Gutenberg's 1448 "invention." In any case, books filled libraries and millions of memos were handwritten before the first practical typewriter was produced by Remington in 1868. Offices bought them, and women, who were considered to have superior manual dexterity, were hired to operate them. Perhaps their dexterity was too great: Early typewriter mechanisms were prone to jamming, so keyboards were designed to slow typists down. Which is how we inherited QWERTY, that pesky arrangement that continues to thwart the efficient moving of type.

"I know so little about the typewriter that once I bought a new one because I couldn't change the ribbon on the one I had."

DOROTHY PARKER

Working Paper. Some of the earliest surviving paper was placed in temples in A.D. 770 by the Empress Shotoku of Japan. She used tiny scrolls, one and a half inches long, to print her "Million Charms"— prayers of thanks because her people had been spared from a plague. Perhaps our working papers aren't as significant—or as charmed—as those of the ancient Empress, but it sure feels like we produce a million of them. They come in all forms: legal pads, business cards, kraft envelopes, Rolodex cards, printed pink sheets that read, "WHILE YOU WERE OUT." These are the sturdy mules of the office, built for cheap speed. They're swell pals, but permanent records should be drawn on better stuff. While not as fugitive as, say, flash paper—the choice of bookies—fax paper is chemically treated and its images fade away with time. Newsprint is even worse. Just ask collectors of Franz Kline's work: In the 1950s the artist did a series of ink wash paintings on newsprint. The paper has since turned orange.

Journals and Diaries. Overstuffed files, stacks of backup disks, boxes of paid bills and canceled checks—they're all about the past. Date books are about the future. If Aunt Pearl's birthday is next Tuesday, the Filofax and Day Runner will remind you to send a card, give you her address, telephone number, shoe size, and keep you within your budget. High-concept date books are like a wildly efficient secretary that one becomes instantly, hopelessly dependent upon. Simpler books have more literary ambitions, and offer pristine pages, free from time lines and categories, upon which one can freely record the unstructured thoughts of unstructured hours.

"Keep a diary and one day it'll keep you."

MAE WEST

HOTEL ÖSTERREICHISCHER
SALZBURG

Personal Stationery. The ironic thing about monogrammed stationery is that, initials or no, it all looks pretty much the same. If "personal" is what you seek, then discreetly liberate some stationery from the Algonquin, the Beirut Intercontinental, or the MicMac Motel. Then punctuate your letters with lipstick kisses, cologne, and the occasional splash of red wine. Or, best of all, make your own paper.

HOW TO MAKE YOUR OWN PAPER

1. Collect non-coated scrap paper from around the house. Old newspaper will do, as will paper towels, toilet paper, motel stationery, and letterheads from failed businesses. **2.** Shred the various papers and put them together in a blender or food processor. **3.**. Add water, Elmer's glue, and a drop of vanilla extract or other fragrant liquid. **4.** Blend thoroughly until a pulp is formed. **5.** Pour pulp onto a cookie sheet and roll out with a rolling pin, squeezing out excess water as you go. **6.** When the paper is dry enough to handle, clip it and hang it on a clothesline until thoroughly dry. Large sheets are easiest to make and can be cut to size.

> "Only on paper has humanity yet achieved glory, beauty, truth, knowledge, virtue and abiding love."
>
> GEORGE BERNARD SHAW

WASTEPAPER

Paper makes up 41 percent of all the trash produced in the U.S.;
10 percent of all the garbage in the world consists of newsprint.
Its recovery rate is about 30 percent.

Beginnings and Endings. At the desk we start, falter, move from elation to frustration, begin again. Our failure is marked by what we reject. Our triumph is held by what we keep. We collect

WASTEPAPER WASTE
*Paper cannot be recycled indefinitely. With each cycle its
fibers become more broken down, until it's eventually deposited in a
landfill or an incinerator.*

each "yes" until it slowly grows into a picture, a story, a new
whole made from dust and notions. Our desk has been there in
the night, our silent companion, bearing witness and coffee stains.

first aid.

Like parenthood, office management requires a range of skills that will never appear on a résumé. Has your fountain pen exploded on your silk jacket? Is your computer choked with dust? First aid first.

EQUIPMENT DEMYSTIFIED

MAKE THE GRADE

(Hardest/lightest to softest/darkest)

Drawing pencils: HHH, HH, H, HB, B, BB, BBB

Writing pencils: 1, 2, 3

Drawing pencils are graded using the symbols "H," which stands for "hard," and "B," which stands for "black." Generally, draftspeople want hard pencils that can keep a point longer and that have less tendency to smudge. Artists are more often concerned with the blackness of a line and may wish to have a very dark stroke with some natural smudging tendencies, which B, 2B, and 3B pencils provide. Somewhere in between is "HB," a grade that indicates that a lead is both hard and dark.

Pencils designed for writing have a different numeric grading system. A No.1 pencil has a hard lead; a No. 2 pencil is both darker and softer; a No. 3 is darker and softer still.

Though both grading systems are more or less universal, the grades themselves are open to interpretation: One manufacturer's 2H may be another manufacturer's HB.

PENULTIMATES

The priciest over-the-counter ballpoint pen is the Madison Slimline, manufactured by Caran D'Ache. It features 6.35-carat diamonds set in 18-carat gold and retails for $40,000.

In 1988 a Japanese collector paid $2,340,000 for a fountain pen. The French-made instrument was encrusted with 600 gems including emeralds, amethysts, and rubies, and took one year to create.

The number "4810" engraved on the nibs of Mont Blanc pens is the height, in meters, of Mont Blanc, the tallest peak in the Alps.

A Parker Duofold fountain pen was used by the Japanese to surrender to Gen. Douglas MacArthur during World War II. Today the same pen retails for $275.

In 1994, Israeli Prime Minister Yitzhak Rabin signed the historic PLO document with a $1.79 Pilot Precise roller ball.

HE LIKED PANE
A hotel in Stirling, Scotland, maintains a Robert Burns Suite because the poet once composed verse on the room's windowpanes, using his diamond ring as a "pen."

POINT OF PURCHASE
Marcel Bich, founder of the BIC Corporation, described his early plastic-bodied ballpoint pens as "a terrible mess. They stain the clothes and they don't write." By 1949 he had refined his product and launched it with a campaign slogan: "It runs. It runs." Within two years, BIC was selling 42 million pens annually.

SERENDIPITY

Standard desk height is 30 inches. Standard typewriter/computer table height is 26 inches. Two-drawer filing cabinets are anywhere from 27 to 29 inches tall. So filing cabinets, smack in between ideal desk and computer table heights, are darn near perfect as the base for a slab desk.

Foot-candle: a unit equivalent to the illumination produced by a source of one candle at a distance of one foot and equal to one lumen incident per square foot.

WORKING LIGHTS

ACTIVITY	FOOT-CANDLE LEVEL		
	LOW	MEDIUM	HIGH
Brief or easy reading	25	50	75
Usual office work	50	75	100
Drawing work with small details and poor contrast	100	150	200
Computer room	25	50	75
Conference room	25	50	75

KNEELING PRETTY

The Balans is a backless kneeling chair that displaces pressure from the spine. Although the design is theoretically sound, it's been shown that people tend to slouch in backless chairs. A standard model that tilts forward may be a better choice.

IS THERE ANYONE OUT THERE?

HELLO, HELLO

The Delaney sisters, authors of Having Our
Say, *have inadvertently set down new rules:
It's now okay for anyone over the age of 100
not to have a telephone. But anyone under
100 must have both a telephone and an
answering machine. Because, without
anyone's really noticing, it has become rude
not to. To a caller an endless ring is more
than annoying, it's alarming. It indicates
that something is terribly wrong: The business
has gone under. Someone has left town, or
yanked the phone from the wall. Worse: You
can't leave a message and will have to keep
trying. It's almost as upsetting as a busy
signal. By comparison, who can complain
about call waiting?*

AT THE SOUND OF THE TONE,
LEAVE YOUR CALLING CARD

*According to Miss Manners, the answering
machine is "the modern equivalent of the
butler, who makes peaceful domestic life
possible by saying, 'Madam is not available;
may I tell her who called?' when Madam is
busy fighting a knot in her needlework or
nursing a hangover."*

ANSWERING MACHINE
ETIQUETTE

THE PERFECT CALLER...

*1. Is never so presumptuous as to say,
"Hi, it's me," even if he or she is married
to the callee. 2. Never demands, "Pick up,"
realizing that the callee would have already
done so if he or she wished to. 3. Doesn't
call in the a.m. and bellow, "You can't be
sleeping, you bum! It's 7:30 already!"
4. Refrains from making disparaging
comments about the welcoming message
such as, "Wow, real original," or, "You
sound like Lucille Ball on a bad day."
5. Realizes that the callee may be accessing
messages from out of town and therefore
doesn't describe in detail every dream he
or she had during the past week. 6. Leaves
a name, general time of call, and specific
reason for calling.*

THE PERFECT CALLEE...

*1. Records a brief identifying message that
assures callers they've reached the correct
party. 2. Doesn't underestimate the caller by
stating the obvious ("I can't take your call
right now...") or leaving elementary
instructions ("leave your name, the date...").
3. Would never bore the caller with obscure,
self-indulgent musical selections followed by
readings of unpublished poetry. 4. Picks up
the minute he or she hears your voice.*

BUILDING A BETTER KEYBOARD

Not all technological improvements are about smaller machines with bigger memories; some computer innovators have turned their attention toward designs that increase users' comfort and reduce risk of injury.

Apple's Adjustable Keyboard, introduced in 1993, is split in half and features an oversized space bar, a separate numeric keyboard, and rounded wrist rests.

The Ullman Keyboard is shaped like an inverted V and is designed to be held in the user's lap.

The Bat, made by Infogrip, has only seven keys and requires the user to press combinations of keys, a process called "chording."

The Datahand, from Industrial Innovations, also employs chording but has no keys at all— it features hand-shaped rests and recessed switches under each finger indentation.

INTERNATIONAL LITERACY

Japanese computers must be far more powerful than Western models. They not only have to accommodate the language's 7,000 symbols but Japanese characters can require as many as 576 dots of light to be seen clearly on a monitor—English characters require as few as 35.

ROLL WITH IT

When you think about it, what's a Rolodex but a seriously analog computer? Although they're now made in electronic models, the classic Rolodex is still the prime tool of shakers, schmoozers, and socialites. And now, for folks on the run, the Rolodex is also available in a portable model that folds up into a neat package with a carrying handle.

FAIR WARNINGS

DISK RISK
When labeling disks, don't use a pencil. Graphite has a slight electrical charge and if graphite residuals get into the "door" of your disk it can crash your data.

TENANT RIGHTS?
Floor-to-ceiling bookcases, anchored to the wall, can be a dramatic and oh-so-useful addition to any office. But if you are a renter, remember that your landlord may be able to claim them as a permanent feature of the apartment or office space.

IT'S MORE THAN A BUSINESS MACHINE, IT'S AN ACCESSORY...RIGHT?
High-end restaurants and theaters in Los Angeles and Miami have begun requiring patrons to check their portable cellular phones at the door.

FILE THIS AWAY

Unless you and your coworkers are professional basketball players, avoid vertical filing cabinets that have more than five drawers.

When setting up office in China, remember that the Chinese language has no alphabet and therefore no logical system for organizing filing systems—or dictionaries and encyclopedias, for that matter.

INK'S MURDER

A leaking ballpoint pen ruins everything. Well, not quite. You can remove those stains by spraying them with cheap aerosol hair spray then rubbing them clean. Or try a full-strength dose of rubbing alcohol. Try soaking larger stains in methyl alcohol for 15 to 30 minutes (that is, unless your garment is made from rayon or acetate, which has to be dry-cleaned). For stains from a marker pen, try rinsing with cold water, placing the fabric on a paper towel and saturating it with alcohol, using a cotton ball as a blotter. Change the paper towel as it absorbs color; then wash the garment in hot water with a laundry detergent and powdered bleach.

MAIL CALL

"...there are certain people whom one almost feels inclined to urge to hurry up and die so that their letters can be published."
CHRISTOPHER MORLEY

EXCELLENT EXCUSES FOR NOT ANSWERING LETTERS SOONER

"The mornings have been cold, the pencil has not been near enough, the paper has been too virgin to deflower, and my own incorrigible laziness has made me postpone, time upon time, the pleasure of continuing our correspondence."
DYLAN THOMAS

"I once started a letter to you...but it dried up and got crumbly. Later I started another, but it got wet and moldy. I intend to get this one down on the floor with my knees on it and push it into an envelope even if it's got maggots."
E. B. WHITE

INITIAL INVESTMENT

Authentic cutout-die monograms are stamped on individual sheets of paper, pierced by hand, and then handpainted—which explains why the best monogrammed stationery can cost upward of $6 per sheet.

THE PLEASURE OF THEIR CO.

Tiffany & Co. will refuse wedding invitation orders unless they are to be engraved in black on ecru or white.

CACHET

Crane's, whose social stationery has graced desktops for nearly 200 years, also supplies the U.S. Government with the rag paper on which money is printed.

where. A desk top is more than the top of a desk, it's things—cool objects which absorb your attention during periods of thought or procastination. Here's some help finding them.

FREEDOM OF CHOICE

Even as the world shrinks and chain stores expand globally, there are plenty of locales where choice is limited if there is any choice at all. However, most manufacturers today can aid you in finding a store or even mail direct to you. The U.S. numbers listed below will help give you freedom of choice.

ORGANIZATIONAL SOFTWARE

Address Express, CoStar Corp.	800/426-9700
Address Writer, CoStar Corp.	800/426-9700
Calendar Creator Plus, Misco/Power Up	800/851-2917
Expense It!, On the Go Software	619/546-4340
FastTrack Schedule, AEC Software	800/346-9413
ManagePro, Avantos Performance Systems, Inc.	800/282-6867
Packrat 5.0, Polaris Software	800/722-5728
Project Scheduler, Scitor Corp.	415/570-7700
Sharkware, CogniTech Corp.	800/947-5075
Time Plus, Day Runner Inc.	800/232-9786
Timeslips, Timeslips Corp.	800/285-0999

PERSONAL ORGANIZERS/HARDWARE

Casio	201/361-5400
Psion	508/371-0310
Rolodex/Tele-Art	818/508-4400
Royal	800/243-3234
Seiko	800/873-4508
Sharp	800/321-8877
Selectronics	716/248-3875

PEN PALS

Cross	800/282-7677
Fisher	800/333-0580
Fujiyama	800/888-9920
Sheaffer	800/346-3736
Waterman	800/523-2486
Mont Blanc	800/877-4810
Parker	800/237-8736
Pelikan	800/874-5898
Quill	800/225-1250
Voyager	800/888-9920

United States

CONNETICUT

BIC CORPORATION
500 Bic Drive
Milford, CT 06460
203/783-2000

FILOFAX, INC.
Merritt #7 Corporate Park
Building 101
Norwalk, CT 06851
203/846-6520
(Leather agendas/organizers)

ILLINOIS

AUTOMATIC, INC.
1238 South Ashland Avenue
Chicago, IL 60608
312/733-6777
*(Full line commercial and
residential furniture)*

MASSACHUSETTS

SHAKER WORKSHOPS
P.O. Box 1028
Concord, MA 01742
617/646-8985
(Shaker reproductions)

MICHIGAN

THOS. MOSER
HERMAN MILLER, INC.
855 East Main Avenue
P.O. Box 302
Zeeland, MI 49464
616/772-3300

NEW JERSEY

EBERHARD FABER,
INC.
4 Century Drive
Parsippany, NJ 07054
201/539-4111
(Uni-ball)

NEW YORK

ABC CARPET & HOME
888 Broadway
New York, NY 10003
212/473-3000
*(Antique, reproduction, and
contemporary furnishings)*

AD HOC SOFTWARES
410 West Broadway
New York, NY 10012
212/925-2652
(Home accessories)

ALFRED DUNHILL
450 Park Avenue
New York, NY 10022
212/753-9292
(Desk accessories, humidors)

ASPREY
725 Fifth Avenue
New York, NY 10022
212/688-1811
(Antiques, desk accessories)

BARNEYS
660 Madison Ave.
New York, NY 10022
212/826-8900
(Stationery, desk accessories)

CARTIER
653 Fifth Avenue
New York, NY 10022
212/446-3459
*(Leather goods, writing
instruments, and stationery)*

C.I.T.E. DESIGN
100 Wooster Street
New York, NY 10012
212/431-7272
*(New and antique furniture
and accessories)*

THE COACH STORE
710 Madison Avenue
New York, NY 10021
212/319-1772 or 800/262-2411

COOPER-HEWITT
NATIONAL MUSEUM OF
DESIGN
2 East 91st Street
New York, NY 10128
212/860-6878
*(Gift shop with home
furnishings)*

DAKOTA JACKSON
306 East 61st Street
New York, NY 10021
212/838-9444
(Contemporary furnishings)

FELISSIMO
10 West 56th Street
New York, NY 10019
212/956-4438
*(Environmentally correct
stationery, decorative objects)*

GALLERY 532
117 Wooster Street
New York, NY 10012
212/219-1327
*(Original American arts and
crafts furniture)*

GHURKA
41 East 57th Street
New York, NY 10022
212/826-8300
(Leather desk accessories)

GUCCI
685 Fifth Avenue
New York, NY 10022
212/826-2600 or
201/867-8800 for national
store listings
(Fine leather desk accessories)

HERMÈS
11 East 57th Street
New York, NY 10022
212/751-3181 or
800/441-4488 for U.S.
listings
*(Fine leather goods, desk
accessories)*

HOPE & WILDER
454 Broome Street
New York, NY 10012
212/966-9010
(Antiques, vintage textiles)

KATE'S PAPERIE
561 Broadway
New York, NY 10012
212/941-9816
*(Paper storage boxes,
stationery)*

THE KNOLL GROUP
105 Wooster Street
New York, NY 10012
212/343-4000
(Modern classics)

L. & J. G. STICKLEY
1 Stickley Drive
P.O. Box 480
Manlius, NY 13104
315/682-5500
*(Reproduction arts and crafts
furniture)*

LOST CITY ARTS
275 Lafayette
New York, NY 10012
212/941-8025
*(American antiquities from the
1920s–60s)*

LUXO CORPORATION
36 Midland Avenue
Port Chester, NY 10573
914/937-4433

METROPOLITAN
MUSEUM OF ART
MUSEUM SHOPS
Fifth Avenue and 82nd
Street
New York, NY 10028
212/535-7710

MICROCOMPUTER
PUBLISHING CENTER,
INC.
4 West 20th Street
New York, NY 10011
212/463-8585
*(Computer hardware and
software)*

MODERN AGE
121 Greene Street
New York, NY 10012
212/477-2224
*(European contemporary
furniture and accessories)*

MUSEUM OF MODERN
ART DESIGN STORE
44 West 53rd Street
New York, NY 10019
212/767-1050 or
800/447-MOMA
(Decorative objects)
Catalogue / Mail Order

NUOVO MELODROM
60 Greene Street
New York, NY 10012
212/219-0013
(Bauhaus furniture)

PACE COLLECTION
986 Madison Avenue
New York, NY 10021
212/535-9616
(Contemporary furnishings)

PALAZZETTI
515 Madison Avenue
New York, NY 10022
212/832-1199
(Contemporary furnishings)

PORTICO
379 West Broadway
New York, NY 10012
212/941-7800
(Home furnishings)

PURE MÄDDERLAKE
478 Broadway
New York, NY 10013
212/941-7770
(Home accessories)

RIZZOLI BOOKSTORE
31 West 57th Street
New York, NY 10019
212/759-2424 or
800/52-BOOKS for U.S.
listings
*(Speialcy books, stationery,
art objects, and fine gift items)*

SAM FLAX
12 West 20th Street
New York, NY 10011
212/620-3038 or
800/726-3529
(Office products)

SAMMY'S
484 Broome Street
New York, NY 10013
212/343-2357
(Rustic antiques and knickknacks)

SENTIMENTO
14 West 55th Street
New York, NY 10019
212/245-3111
(Antique decorative objects)

SONY ELECTRONIC
STORE
550 Madison Avenue
New York, NY 10022
212/833-8800
(State-of-the-art electronic
merchandise and goods)

STAPLES
1075 Avenue of the Americas
New York, NY 10018
212/944-6791 or
800/333-3330 for store
nearest you
(Office supplies, storage boxes)

TAKASHIMAYA
693 Fifth Avenue
New York, NY 10022
212/350-0100
(Home furnishings,
stationery)

TERRA VERDE
120 Wooster Street
New York, NY 10012
212/925-4533
(Ecological home furnishings)

TIFFANY & CO.
727 Fifth Avenue
New York, NY 10022
212/755-8000 or
800/526-0649
(Fine desk accessories, leather
goods, stationery, and pens)

ZONA
97 Greene Street
New York, NY 10012
212/925-6750
(Imported and domestic
decorative accessories)

PENNSYLVANIA

DAY-TIMERS, INC.
Allentown, PA 18001
215/395-5884 for catalogue
of products
(Personal planning systems
and office products)

UTAH

PORSCHE DESIGN
331 South Rio Grande
Suite 105
Salt Lake City, UT 84101
800/521-5152
(Writing instruments)

**CATALOGUE/MAIL
ORDER**

A. T. CROSS COMPANY
1 Albion Road
Lincoln, RI 02865
401/333-1200 or
800/AT Cross
(Writing instruments, desk
sets, and accessories)

APPLE COMPUTER, INC.
1 Infinite Loop
Cupertino, CA 95014
800/776-2333 for
information on Apple
products, programs
(Computers)

FOUNTAIN PEN
HOSPITAL
10 Warren Street
New York, NY 10007
212/964-0580 or
800/253-PENS
(Writing instruments and
inkwells)

IKEA
1000 Center Drive
Elizabeth, NJ 07202
908/289-4488 or
412/747-0747 for East Coast
listings or
818/842-4532 for West Coast
listings
(Desk and office furniture)

MONT BLANC USA
75 North Street
Bloomsbury, NJ 08804
800/995-4810
(Fine writing instruments)

REMO MAIL-ORDER
CATALOGUE
Oxford at Crown Street
Sydney, Australia
8/029-714
(Hip general store)

2 WOMEN BOXING
3002B Commerce Street
Dallas, TX 75226
214/939-1626
(Stationery and photo albums)

INTERNATIONAL
LISTINGS

France

PARIS

ALFRED DUNHILL
15, rue de la Paix
75002
42/61-57-58
(Cigar boxes, desk accessories)

CALLIGRANE
4 & 6, rue du Pont-Louis-
Philippe
75004
48/04-31-89 or 40/27-00-74
(Desk and paper products)

GUCCI
2, rue du Faubourg-Saint-
Honoré
75008
42/96-83-27
*(Desk accessories, agendas,
and leather and porcelain
boxes)*

HERMÈS
24, rue du Faubourg-Saint-
Honoré
75008
40/17-47-17
*(Fine leather goods, furniture,
and desk accessories)*

PAPIER PLUS
9, rue du Pont-Louis-
Philippe
75004
42/77-70-49
*(Quality stationery, paper
articles, and blank notebooks)*

STERN
47, passage des Panoramas
75002
45/08-86-45
*(Engravers since 1840;
traditional invitations,
calling cards)*

Great Britain

LONDON

AERO
96 Westbourne Grove
W2
71/221-1950
*(Modern and contemporary
furniture and accessories)*

ALFRED DUNHILL OF
LONDON LTD.
30 Duke Street
71/499-9566
(Fine desk accessories)

AMERICAN RETRO
35 Old Compton Street
W1
71/734-3477
(Decorative items for the home)

ASPREY
165 New Bond Street
W1
71/493-6767
(Desk accessories)

THE CONRAN SHOP
Michelin House
81 Fulham Road
SW3
71/589-7401
(Home furnishings)

DIDIER AARON LTD.
21 Ryder Street
71/839-4716
(Antiques)

THE FILOFAX CENTRE
21 Conduit Street
W1
71/499-0457
(Personal organizers)

THE GENERAL
TRADING COMPANY
144 Sloane Street
SW1X 9BL
71/730-0411
(Stationery, Filofax)

IKEA LTD
2 Drury Way
North Circular Road
NW10 0TH
81/451-5566

ITALIAN PAPER SHOP
11 Brompton Arcade
SW3
71/589-1668
*(Florentine paper and marbled
paper from the Netherlands)*

LEFAX
28-32 Shelton Street
WC2
71/836-1977
*(Personal organizers in
various leathers and vinyl)*

FREUD'S
198 Shaftesbury Avenue
WC2
71/831-1071
*(Lighting and home
accessories)*

THE LONDON
LIGHTING CO.
135 Fulham Road
SW3
71/589-3612
(Modern lighting designs)

MUJI
26 Great Marlborough
Street
W1V 1HB
71/494-1197
(No-name products)

PAPERCHASE
213 Tottenham Court Road
W1
71/580-8496
(Paper boxes, stationery)

PENCRAFT
91 Kingsway
WC2
71/405-3639
*(Pens by Mont Blanc, Parker,
Waterman, and Sheaffer)*

SMYTHSON OF BOND
STREET
44 New Bond Street
W1
71/629-8558
*(Notepads, ledgers, and
Florentine marbled paper)*

SOTHEBY'S
34-35 New Bond Street
W1
71/493-8080
*(Auction house specializing in
antiques and furniture)*

Italy

FLORENCE

GIANNI E FIGLIO
Piazza Pitti 37
50123
55/21-26-21
(*The grandfather of all paper shops, founded in 1856*)

IL PAPIRO
Via Cavour 55
50123
55/21-52-62
(*Marbled papers made in Florence*)

MILAN

STANDARD
Via Legnano, 28
20121
2/290-01-110
(*Home furniture and accessories, lighting*)

ROME

CASSINA
Via del Babuino 100-101
00168
6/79-33-30
(*Architect-designed furniture*)

LABORATORIO
SCATOLE
Via della Stelletta 27
00168
6/880-20-53
(*Marbled notebooks, writing paper, files, and boxes*)

PAPIRUS
Via Capo Le Case 55A
00168
6/78-04-18
(*Boxes, papercraft, and desk items*)

PINEIDER
Via dei Due Macelli 68
00168
6/78-90-13
(*Stationery, leather-bound desk diaries*)

Japan

TOKYO

IN THE ROOM
1-12-13 Jin-nan
Shibuya-ku 150
03/3464-0101
(*Large home furniture store with desks, home electronics*)

INNOVATOR
1-4-7 Kita-Aoyama
Minato-ku 107
03/3403-7544
(*Swedish-designed simple and functional desks*)

ITOYA
2-7-15 Ginza
Chuo-ku 104
03/3561-8311
(*Specialty store of stationery from around the world*)

LOFT
21-1 Udagawacho
Shibuya-ku 150
03/3462-0111
(*Desks, desk accessories*)

TOKYU HANDS
12-18 Udagawacho
Shibuya-ku 150
03/5489-5111
(*Large store with desks and practical furniture*)

TREASURE HOUSE
WATANABE
3-24-3 Soshigaya
Setagaya-ku 157
03/3483-0015
(*High-grade furniture with a selection of escritoires [writing desks]*)

RESOURCES

JACKET FRONT

DESK LAMP - C.I.T.E.; **INK BOTTLE** - Kate's Paperie; **STATIONERY** - Terra Verde; Toledo **ALUMINUM CHAIR** - The Knoll Group; Streamerica **FOUNTAIN PEN** and **STAND** - Tiffany & Co.

BACK

ANTIQUE TYPEWRITER - State Supply Equipment and Props, Inc.

DESK

10 **TABLES** (top) Anita Calero collection; (bottom) ABC Carpet and Home

15 **DESK/CHAIR** - State Supply Equipment and Props, Inc.

17 **BOOKS** - Zona; **COLORED PENCILS AND PAPER CLIPS** - Terra Verde

18 Arts and crafts **DESK** and **STICKLEY CHAIR** - both from Gallery 532

23 **COMPUTER STAND** - Power Wagon by Automatic, Inc.; **CHAIR** - Nuovo Melodrum

26 Elsa Peretti Sterling silver **PEN** - Tiffany & Co.; **STATIONERY** and **ENVELOPES** - Terra Verde; **BRIEFCASE** - Sally Schneider collection

27 **NEWTON** - Microcomputer Publishing Center, Inc.

31 Apple **POWER BOOK** Duo - Jeff Stone collection

34 **NOTEBOOK** and **FOUNTAIN PEN** - Kate's Paperie; **ANTIQUE POSTCARDS** - Pure Madderlake

WORK SPACE

36 **DESK LAMP** - C.I.T.E.; **INK BOTTLE** - Kate's Paperie; **STATIONERY** - Terra Verde; Toledo **ALUMINUM CHAIR** - The Knoll Group; Streamerica **FOUNTAIN PEN** and **STAND** - Tiffany & Co.

38 Keyboard **WRIST PADS** - MOMA Design Store

39 **MEDALLION** - Anita Calero collection; **PAGE** from *Architectural Graphic Standards*, 8th Edition, published by John Wiley & Sons - David Gross collection

40 Antique **TABLE** and **CHAIR** - ABC Carpet & Home; **WIRE BOWL** - Zona; **GLASS BOTTLE** - Hope and Wilder

44 **BANKER'S CHAIR** - Julian Richards collection

45 **OFFICE CHAIR** - The Knoll Group

46–47 **UNI-BALL PEN** - Chic Simple collection

48 **TABLE** - ABC Carpet and Home; **TABLE TOP OBJECTS** - Anita Calero collection

50–51 **LUXO LAMP** - Sam Flax
52 **STATIONERY** - Kate's Paperie;
Sterling silver **TRIANGLE DISH** -
available at MOMA; **INK BOTTLE**
with flower print - Terra Verde;
INK TIP REFILLS - Kate's Paperie; Elsa
Peretti Sterling silver **PEN** - Tiffany & Co.;
Magnifying glass **LETTER OPENER** - Zona;
PAPER CLIPS - Terra Verde
54 (upper left) **GLASS VASE** - Ad Hoc
Softwares; Paper **FOLDER FILE** - Kate's
Paperie; (lower right) **ANTIQUE CHAIR** -
ABC Carpet & Home; **BOXES** - Kate's
Paperie and Terra Verde
55 (upper left) **PYREX MEDICINE JAR** -
C.I.T.E.; **MEASURING CONTAINERS** -
Ad Hoc Software; Elsa Peretti Sterling
silver **PEN** - Tiffany & Co.; **TORTOISE
PEN** - Takashimaya; **WOOD FRAME** -
Sammy's; (lower right) **SHAKER BOXES** -
Shaker Workshops, Arlington, Mass.;
TOLEDO CHAIR - The Knoll Group
58 **TEA BOX** - Takashimaya

EQUIPMENT

62 **PAPER WEIGHT WITH CLIP** - Sally
Schneider collection
64–65 **PENCILS, PAPER CLIPS** and **CIRCULAR
CLIPS, SCOTCH TAPE, INK BOTTLE** -
Terra Verde; Fountain pen **TIP REFILLS** -
Kate's Paperie
66–67 **SLAB TABLE, DESK ACCESSORIES,
CHAIR** - Sally Schneider collection
68–69 **STATIONERY** - Felissimo
70 **PENS** (left to right): **FOUNTAIN PEN** -
Tiffany & Co.; **FELT TIP MARKER** - Chic
Simple collection; **BALLPOINT PEN** -
MOMA Design Store; **GLASS JAR** - Ad
Hoc Softwares
72–73 **FOUNTAIN PENS** - The Fountain Pen
Hospital Office Supplies
75 **INKS** - Kate's Paperie
77 **ANTIQUE TYPEWRITER** - State Supply
Equipment and Props, Inc.
79 **STATIONERY** - Felissimo
80 **JOURNALS** - all except bottom from
Rizzoli International; (bottom) **FILOFAX** -
Dana Gallagher collection
82–83 **HOTEL STATIONERY** - Anita Calero
collection
84–85 **PAPER** (left to right) yellow pad, white
pad, quad-rule graph paper - collection of
Chic Simple

QUOTES

2 **CHINESE PROVERB,** *The Columbia Dictionary of Quotations* (Columbia University Press, 1993).

8 **AUSTRALIAN ABORIGINAL SAYING**

11 **FLAUBERT,** *Freelance Forever* (Avon, 1982).

13 **DOROTHY PARKER,** *The Columbia Dictionary of Quotations* (Columbia University Press, 1993).

14 **MR. NORTON,** *The Wall Street Journal Book of Chief Executive Style* (William Morrow, 1989).

21 *The Rocky Horror Picture Show,* 1975.

22 **CYNTHIA HEIMEL,** *But Enough About You* (Simon & Schuster, 1986).

25 **AGATHA CHRISTIE,** *Writers on Writing* (Running Press, 1990).

30 **PABLO PICASSO,** *1,911 Best Things Anybody Ever Said* (Ballantine Books, 1988).

37 **WILLIAM FAULKNER,** *Writers on Writing* (Running Press, 1990).

53 **WILLIAM BLAKE,** *The Harper Book of Quotations,* Third Edition (HarperCollins, 1993).

63 **OWEN EDWARDS,** *Elegant Solutions: Quintessential Technology for a User-Friendly World* (Crown, 1989).

72–73 **JOHN MIDDLETON MURRY,** quoted in *The Pencil: A History of Design and Circumstance,* by Henry Petroski (Alfred A. Knopf, 1990).

74 **HENRY PETROSKI,** *The Pencil: A History of Design and Circumstance* (Alfred A. Knopf, 1990).

76 **DOROTHY PARKER,** *Writers on Writing* (Running Press, 1990).

81 **MAE WEST,** *The Penguin Dictionary of Modern Humorous Quotations* (Penguin Books, 1986).

83 **GEORGE BERNARD SHAW,** quoted in *A Treasury of the World's Great Letters,* edited by M. Lincoln Schuster (Simon & Schuster, 1940–1968).

104 **WALT WHITMAN,** preface to *Leaves of Grass,* 1860.

ACKNOWLEDGMENTS

STYLE CONSULTANT	Anita Colero
MANUFACTURER & RETAIL RESEARCH	Susan Claire Maloney
QUOTE RESEARCH	Lige Rushing & Kate Doyle Hooper
COPY EDITING	Borden Elniff

AND SPECIAL THANKS TO: C. Daniel Bergfeld of the Luxo Corporation, Lauren Clarke Caldwell, Tony Chirico, M. Scott Cookson, Kreon Cyros of the Massachusetts Institute of Technology, Bia Da Costa, Lauri Del Commune, Michael Drazen, Deborah Freeman, Jane Friedman, Hayward Hill Gatling, Janice Goldklang, Jo-Anne Harrison, Patrick Higgins, Katherine Hourigan, Andy Hughes, Carol Janeway, Barbara Jones-Diggs, Nicholas Latimer, William Loverd, Anne McCormick, Dwyer McIntosh, Sonny Mehta, Amy Needle, Lan Nguyen, Julian Richards, Sally Schneider, Sandra J. Shea, Anne-Lise Spitzer, Robin Swados, Aileen Tse, Shelley Wanger, Cecil Williams of Herman Miller, Inc.

COMMUNICATIONS

The world has gotten smaller and faster but we still can only be in one place at a time, which is why we are anxious to hear from you. We would like your input on stores and products that have impressed you. We are always happy to answer any questions you have about items in the book, and of course we are interested in feedback about Chic Simple.

Our address is:
84 WOOSTER STREET • NEW YORK, NY 10012
Fax (212)343-9678
Email address: **info@chicsimple.com**
Compuserve number: **72704,2346**

Stay in touch because "The more you know, the less you need."

KIM JOHNSON GROSS & JEFF STONE

TYPE

The text of this book was set in two typefaces: New Baskerville and Futura.

The ITC version of **NEW BASKERVILLE** is called Baskerville, which itself is a facsimile reproduction of types cast from molds made by John Baskerville (1706–1775) from his designs. Baskerville's original face was one of the forerunners of the typestyle known to printers as the "modern face"—a "modern" of the period A.D. 1800. **FUTURA** was produced in 1928 by Paul Renner (1878–1956), former director of the Munich School of Design, for the Bauer Type Foundry. Futura is simple in design and wonderfully restful in reading. It has been widely used in advertising because of its even, modern appearance in mass and its harmony with a great variety of other modern types.

SEPARATION AND FILM PREPARATION BY

DIGITAL PRE-PRESS, INC.

New York, New York

PRINTED AND BOUND BY

BERTELSMANN PRINTING AND MANUFACTURING CORP.

Berryville, Virginia

HARDWARE

Apple Macintosh Quadra 700 and 800 personal computers; APS Technologies Syquest Drives; MicroNet DAT Drive; SuperMac 21" Color Monitor; Radius PrecisionColor Display/20; Radius 24X series Video Board; Hewlett-Packard LaserJet 4, Supra Fax Modem

SOFTWARE

QuarkXPress 3.3, Adobe Photoshop 2.5.1, Microsoft Word 5.1, FileMaker Pro 2.0, Adobe Illustrator 5.0.1

MUSICWARE

Johnny Cash *(Cash)*, Sarah McLachlan *(Fumbling Towards Ecstasy)*, Beastie Boys *(Ill Communication)*, Ray Lynch *(Nothing Above My Shoulders but the Evening)*, Dead Can Dance *(Into the Labyrinth)*, The Clash *(London Calling)*, Milt Jackson *(The Prophet Speaks)*, The Modern Jazz Quartet *(MJQ40/Disc Three)*, The Replacements *(All Shook Down)*, Miles Davis *(In A Silent Way)*, Axia *(Vol. 1)*, The Best of The Velvet Underground *(Words and Music of Lou Reed)*

"The art of art, the glory of expression and the sunshine of the light of letters, is simplicity."

WALT WHITMAN